Paper Words
and
Paper Hearts

Selected Poems by Pallavi Kumbla

I would like to thank my parents, Lakshmikantha and Anju Kumbla, and my sister, Anjali, and all my friends who supported me in my endeavors to write these poems.

Table of Contents

Additional Poems

1 ("Dreams")
Dreams keep us going,
Going to the point of reaching something intangible.
Can they ever be reached?
It's an unanswerable question.

We dream of things we want.
I dream of people lost, times past, times to regain—
All things I WANT but can't seem to get,
At least not now.

Maybe it's good that dreams don't come true.
Their motivation keeps us sane,
Their motivation keeps us suffering—
Nothing is gained without pain.

Dreams remembered are painful,
Simply because they are never real,
Teasing and torturing
Until time heals all wounds.

But should we wish dreams away?
It's an unanswerable question.
I'll wait for answers,
Until the end of time—
Waiting...
Just simply waiting...

2 ("Forgotten")
What brings people together?
What tears people apart?
I ponder this question often.
How is it so easy for some to drop others,
As if they were disposable,
While keeping others who do not even try?

Do those who drop
Know what it feels like to be forgotten?
If they did, would they reclaim those lost in their wrath?
Do those deserted drop others
Who have hurt them?

It is an endless, vicious cycle.
I wonder if those who dropped so easily
Think of those they forgot?
I think of those people who so easily
Erased me—
At least once every day.

I pray to be reunited with them.
But is that the best thing?
A strained relationship will always be strained.
I should move on I know,
But TIME ticks too slowly by
For me to let go now.

Maybe in the next second
I will let go…
I just don't know.

3 ("Pain")
Why do people feel?
A simple question,
Yet so hard to answer.

We say "pain is mental."
Yet, we *feel* pain
So harshly.

Is the negative connotation of pain
So mental that it turns physical?
Or, do we really feel?

We treat pain —
A whole industry devoted to it.
But pain can never be treated —
An elusive phantom.
It's what makes us real.
It's what makes us human.

Would I take pain out of my life?
Ask me when I'm in pain —
I'll say yes.
No surprise there.
Ask me when I'm not in pain —
I'll say yes.
No surprise there.

But, I *feel* that it constitutes a part of me.
Take it away, and I have not learned,
Not grown.
Take it away, and I would simply exist...
Nothing else.

4 ("Good People")
I met a good person today.
It always catches me off guard.
Good people aren't hard to come by,
Keeping them is.

Catch them,
Net them,
Don't let them go,
Because retaining the next one
Will be even harder.

Meteors—
Once in a lifetime.
People line up,
Telescopes in hand,
Only to CATCH a glimpse
Of something gone by quickly.
Good people are like meteors—
Only if you let them pass by too quickly.

Fish—
Hard to NET.
But once done,
A swarm of pleasure drowns one.
Good people are like fish—
Only in the fact that one
Must hold on to them strongly.

Catch good people.
Net good people.
But never blink or lose your grip,
Because like meteors or fish,
They'll be gone—
Leaving you wondering…
What went wrong?

5 ("Dark Youth, White Companion")
I *have* a friend.
We *say* dark youth,
White companion.
Me—
The dark youth.
Her—
The white companion.
Fate brought us together.
Fate tested us.
Betrayal—
Never known.
That's the way it should be.

I *had* a friend
We *said* dark youth,
White companion.
Me—
The dark youth.
Her—
The white companion.
Fate brought us together.
Fate tested us.
Betrayal—
Sadly known.
A capsule of memories—
Mostly good.
That's all I have left.

6 ("Words")
Words—
Heartfelt.
Words—
Aesthetic.
Words—
So many combinations,
Too many to count.

Words—
Harsh.
Words—
Hurtful.
So *so* many combinations,
Way too many to count.

Words please.
Words catch off guard.
Words bring happiness.
Words bring sadness.
Words bring truth.
Words bring lies.
Words make relationships.
Words break relationships.

Words—
The root of all goodness.
Words—
The root of all evil.
Words—
Do everything.
Words—
Are everything.

7 ("Focus")
I stare at a piece of artwork.
Someone stands next to me.

Aesthetically pleasing—
Yes to me,
Not to the other.

Distraction overcomes me.
I can't focus.
Why are they not pleased?

I really can't focus now.
I just want them to leave.

They stand—
Staring but not getting.

Wait—
My mind—
Induces a self-realization—
Maybe *I* am not getting it.

My brain ponders—
Not about the artwork.

I can't focus.
They focus.
I am not getting it.
I AM NOT GETTING IT.
They are getting it.
THEY ARE GETTING IT.

8 ("Clarity")
Cold breeze—
My face.
Pavement—
My feet.
Air—
My fingers.
Music—
My ears.
All my senses—
In tune,
The most in tune they've ever been.
My mind clear.
My heart beating—
With each beat,
Rush of blood through my arteries.
My lungs heaving—
With each rise,
Rush of air through my lungs.
With each step,
Adrenaline.
A great feeling.

9 ("Decay")
Cold breeze—
My face.
Pavement—
My feet.
Air—
My fingers.
Music—
My ears.
All my senses chaotic,
The most chaotic they've ever been.
My mind opaque.
My heart beating—
With each beat,
A feeling of explosion.
My lungs heaving—
With each rise,
A gasp for oxygen.
With each step,
Muscles decaying.
The end—
So close,
Yet so far.
A great feeling.

10 ("Compassion")
Compassion —
Should be shown to everyone,
But is not.
I hope we are all compassionate,
That it is just dormant.
BRING IT BACK.
BRING IT BACK.

They say —
Think before saying,
Think before acting.
I say —
Think *compassionately* before saying,
Think *compassionately* before acting.

Compassion brings class.
But, not everyone shows class.
Show compassion,
You will show class.
Everyone has potential
To show class.
Compassion is dormant —
Bring it to life.

Compassion —
A concept easily forgotten,
A concept so simple.
STOP,
THINK,
ACT,
Compassionately.

Live life compassionately.

11 ("Bad Days")
Bad days—
Inevitable.
Sucking energy,
And moral.
Thursday was one.
Left and right,
People saying—
"NO!"
"NO!"
"NO!"
"Why?" I ask.
Ears filtering,
"You...
No!"
"Bad behavior...
Yes!"
"Role model...
No!"
I sit,
Stunned.
Soul—
Beat down.
Time passed—
Eternity.
No.
Just one minute.
My hands wet—
Why?
No rain.

Run away?
A good idea.
No.

God takes away,
But gives back.

Looking up,
An image—
Orange fused with pink,
Blue mixed in,
Lights enhancing the image.
I stare,
And think—
God is not teasing.
He's showing me,
Telling me,
OVERCOME.

12 ("Story")
I saw a man.
No one I knew—
Yet,
Special.
Brain bashed in,
Unconscious.
Yet,
He told me
A story.
I listened,
With my eyes.

He said—
Treat *all* with
Love,
Even foes.
Let go.
Hostility—
Show none.
Deception—
Don't practice.

He asked—
Are you
Happy?
Can you say
Tomorrow,
If gone,
You loved all?

I stare
At him,
Blankly.
I say,
Simply say—
No.

Change—
I have to.

He told me
A story.
I listened.

He knows
Not me.
I know
Of him.
Seeing him
Again—
I can't say
I would recognize him.
No name.
No face.
No history,
Except—
Bat to the head.

Simply—
He told me
A story.
I listened.
*I LISTENED,
AND CHANGED.*

13 ("I Love You")
I LOVE YOU.
Three simple words
Said everyday,
But rarely meant...
Until it's too late.
Friends,
Family,
Acquaintances—
Love is
What?

Scenario:
Me—
Passing time.
Beeping of phone.
Other 1: Stop by. You leave tomorrow.
Me: Not a good idea.
Other 2: Not a good idea
Beeping of phone.
Other 1: Please.
Me: No.
Beeping of Phone.
Other 1: *Friend, I love you.*
Me: No. You don't.
Beeping of phone.
Other 1: I need to talk to you.
Me: I can't.
Other 2: Don't.

I left—
Not looking back.

We love
Everyone,
Not realizing.

We love
Even if we resist,
Even if we *hate,*
Even if we never see again.

We love—
Friends,
Family,
Acquaintances,
Foes.

We love—
Everyone.

14 ("You and Me")
Don't talk.
Don't listen.
Don't look—
At *me*,
Or to *me*.

Drifting apart—
A natural course of life.
We did this.
All people do this.

Where time spaced us,
Two others became closer—
Filling the void.

I wondered—
Where did we stand
When time interrupted?
I still wonder—
Where do we stand
Now that time has moved on?

Questions can be answered,
But that will never be closure.
Closure can never be reached—
Not when time has embellished truth,
Not when time has caused the drifting.

This is the last recollection.
I can't get caught in time.
I must move with it,
Even if that means forgetting acquaintances.

15 ("Care Full")
Happiness—
Held in our hands.
My happiness—
In your hands.
Your happiness—
In my hands.
Show responsibility.
Care for me.
I will care back.
Don't care for me.
I will care back.

Human—
Me.
You.
Humane—
Me.
Not you.
Humanity—
(You) Show some.

16 ("Blind")
I see you.
You don't see me.
Your choice.

I welcome your exclusion
With open arms —
It's feeding my persistence.

Don't break my spirit.
Don't stop the ignoring,
Just the ignorance.

Associations are selective.
Ignorance is not —
We can all be ignorant.
We must see beyond it.

Fine —
Ignore me.
Just don't be ignorant of my cause,
Of others' causes.

17 ("Symbiosis")
I'm smart.
I can sense things.
Or, maybe it's just
Words,
Getting back around to me.

Dues—
Paid.
Guilt—
Shed.
I am ready to move on.

But,
I am hindered.
Not by myself—
Not anymore.
But,
By others.

I say
To them—
Look beyond.
See other qualities—
Good ones.
Help me grow.
I will help you grow.
I will learn
From you.
You will learn
From me.
Not a host-parasite relationship.
Rather,
A symbiotic relationship.

18 ("Floaters and Normals")
Floaters—
Different from
Normals.

Floaters—
Practice host-parasite relationships.
Normals—
Practice giving and receiving,
Practice normality.

Not everyone knows a floater—
A good thing.
Everyone knows a normal—
A good thing.
Floaters—
I call them—
Users and Abusers.

Floaters—
Never learn.
It's impossible.
They don't realize
What they are,
Who they are—
Floaters.
There's the first problem.

19 ("Separation")
Not thinking,
I dive.
Arm outstretched—
Shock to the arm.

Not thinking,
I switch from right
To left.
Shock to the arm...
And leg.

Separation between
Body and Mind
Occurs now,
Never at any other time.
Subconscious shut down,
Body totally relying
On its anatomy.
It's peace of mind...
In 15 point intervals.

Pain—
Unnoticeable
To the mind—
It's shutdown.
Pain—
Not known,
Not now.
Everyone should experience this.

20 ("One Day")
If you had one day
To figure out yourself,
How would you do it?
Sit around?
Ask people?
Recollect memories?
A tough situation.

What defines you?—
Things said?
Actions done?
People associated with?
Things owned?
No.
None of these.
It's something more real,
Yet unknown.
It can't be figured out,
Not in one day—
Only in a lifetime,
Whatever that may be to you.

The key—
Patience.

Tough question,
But not futile,
Not irrelevant.
Just time consuming...
And frustrating.

21 ("Tell Me Now")
I blend with the night—
Hood up,
Sleeves down,
I walk stealthily.
I WALK STEALTHILY.
It shouldn't be—
Everyone else uncovered,
Except me.
I've done no wrong.

Cautious—
I'm inside.
Stairs—
I'm up.
Window—
Clear.
I'm in.
Twice done.
I'm good.
It's a shame—
All to help a sick friend.

Tell me now—
Your preconceptions.
Tell me now—
Your domain.
Tell me now—
I am wrong.
I'm doing *your* job.
Where are you?—
Tell me now.

22 ("5")
It counts now.
I must deliver.
Slam down,
I am in the air.
Floating—
3 seconds.
I look down—
One girl,
Three boys,
All with hands up.
I am up.
They down.
Let go—
Not sinking.
I am down,
Really down.
They are down.
No—
Really up.
I need it again.
I must have this feeling again.
I must!
It occurs rarely.
I will get it again tomorrow.
Time slows
Until that moment,
Then speeds off,
But leaving adrenaline
For at least 5 seconds.
I live for that 5.

23 ("Deception")
A collage—
Yet you stand out.
Why?
Is there something special about you?
I think there is.
I just don't know what.
I keep wondering,
But I can never figure it out.
Maybe—
Your personality.
Maybe—
Your facial features.
Or maybe—
Your human nature,
Which I can never figure out,
Nor understand.
Yes.
I think that's it.
Your special feature—
Your nature—
Trustful.
It caught me off guard.
It still does.
It always will.

24 ("Lost Music")
Music brings inspiration.
The way the music is created —
From the mind,
To the fingers
Playing the instrument,
The way the lyrics blend with the beat,
The uniqueness of the vocalist's voice,
All meshes together.

But for me,
When I listen to music,
I see the eyes,
And the brows.
They tell the real story.
The eyes sing the song.
The brows bring the feeling,
And emotion.
Strip away everything.
Go acoustic.
You will see this.

Lyrics are poems.
Eyes are the voice.
Brows are the face,
The mind.
Ears are the audience.
The troubadours of France knew this.
We know this —
It just sometimes gets lost.

25 ("Back to the Basics")
Let's go back to the basics.
Back to a time of exploring
Humanity,
And human interactions.
Remove complexity.
Remove all things of that nature.
Just look at the simple aspects—
At least,
Of life.
Simplicity is complicated.
No easy task.
But it
Must be done.
How?
Make simple observations.
Don't speak.
Don't think.
Just observe.
Observation is all around us.
We just ignore it
For a microscopic view,
Not a macroscopic view.
Let's find *OUR* way home.
We can better *OUR* lives
Together.
Just make at least
ONE observation—
Each individual—
And *WE* will have made
The world's difference.
A united front.

Back to the basics—
A simple concept,
Yet more complicated than any other.

26 ("Immune")
I wonder—
Why did this happen to me?
I always hear of it happening to others.
Immune—
I felt so.
Not anymore.
You think you are prepared for life
And things like this,
But no one ever is,
Really.
I hated the world.
I wondered—
Why me?
What did I do,
For God to wish this Karma upon me.
The hair loss.
The tired voice.
The sunken face.
Too much to bear.
No one understood—
It's not their problem.

I hate the C word.
I always will.
It's hard to say,
And hear.
But it's even harder to say,
"My mom has cancer."
Nothing will change that
Or make it less brutal.
But it will never define a person.
An affliction—
Yes.
Cruel—
Yes.
But it can never beat down

The soul.
Beat down the body—
Yes.
But it is always
Defeatable—
Its weakness,
Like all other human qualities.
Its soon to be ultimate downfall—
As time ticks by
It weakens,
Becomes more defeatable,
Not more bearable.
I'll be there—
In mind,
In spirit,
When cancer is
Defeated.

27 ("Green Colored Paper")
A piece of paper—
Traveled so far.
So many hands,
So many places,
Carrying so many people,
And a piece of them
With it.

I want to know—
What larger group
Am I a part of?
Who am I mingling with?

We are all different,
But connected by this paper.
It's not long in my hands,
But my hands leave a
Permanent mark.

We spend quickly,
Not thinking,
"What has this paper been used for?
Good deeds?
Bad deeds?
Has it helped someone?
Has it hurt someone?"

Money has worth,
Definitely in a double sense.
The obvious—
The number it carries.
The face it holds.
The not so obvious—
The history of its travels,
From the time it was created,
To the time it reached you,

To the time it reached me,
To the time it reached someone else,
To the time it was destroyed.

I don't know you,
But we are connected by this paper.
We always will be.
This is the real value of this paper.

28 ("Cake")
Slam the door in my face—
Cut off all ties—
Don't look at me
EVER again.
I really can't care.

See—
It's your loss.
A lifelong friendship's not worth it.
I'll hide this one,
Or *TWO*
Far underground.
I do want to ask you—
How is life treating you?

See—
I still care about
Your welfare,
But not to see you,
Or hear about
Your actions.

Don't return the favor.
I know you can't.
It's ok.
Just know that
I think of *EVERYONE* I've met.
I just can't *ERASE* people.
You can't either.
You just haven't come to terms with this
FACT.

29 ("Self-Worth")
Understanding the value of self-worth
And that *NO ONE,*
NOT ANYONE
Can take it away,
NOT for a second,
Is the key to living healthy.
It may feel
Like you've been stripped
Of it—
I've felt like that.
But feeling is not being,
And it was never lost.

Control—
Never lost—
Not in my case.
Not in your case.

Self-worth is abstract.
Abstract is protection—
Abstract can't be stolen—
The beauty of it.

People who think they control
Self-worth not of their own
Feel little control over their own.
When they finally realize
They control their own,
They will understand that
Self-worth is intrinsic—
Intrinsic to the person it belongs to.

Self-worth—
Permanently chained to its one.

30 ("Choices")
Choices are choices.
We don't always make
The right ones.
I know I haven't.
I know you didn't.
An acceptable fact.

Choices are choices,
Until they affect another.
Then choices are bitter-sweet.
Bitter at first,
When time punishes.
Sweet later,
When time heals all wounds.

Choices are choices.
It's your choice
To make the right ones.

31 ("Fight!")
In any argument
Two sides exist.
Both sides are wrong.
To blame both sides—
Irresponsible.
Sides don't exist
When both are wrong.
Wars fought.
Friends lost.
Family forgotten.
It's futile,
All futile.
Peace—
Futile.
What we need—
Respect.
To respect each other's
Views,
Opinions,
Not convince others to change—
That creates arguments.
Just respect—
Wars,
Feuds,
Loss,
Death—
All will be avoided.

32 ("Internal Collapse")
Heat waves ahead.
Heat waves behind.
I'm walking,
Walking forever,
To a destination—
None I know.
I don't know where it will end,
If it does.
I hope it doesn't.
You are next to me.
We—
The last two people—
Not talking,
Just walking.
Time passed: forever—
An oasis dries up in this time.
A third person appears.
Only one can go on.
Chosen: You.

The two
Walking away.
I can't move.
I'm on my knees,
Bleeding from my heart.
You—
The reason.
You—
Never thought of me.
You—
Killed me.

33 ("Natural Rebellion")
I want
I want
I WANT
To scream
On a mountaintop
Overlooking a ravine,
But I can't...
Not physically.

I run
I run
I RUN
With scissors
And...and
A lollipop
In my mouth.
Taboo—
Yes.
But I can do
WHATEVER I want—
In my mind.

My freedom—
Stripped physically,
Not in my mind.
My mind—
Flexing.
A renegade.
Liberated.
Pumping.
I scream
On a mountaintop
Overlooking a ravine—
In my mind.

This type of thinking

Could do me in,
Probably will.
But it can't be stolen—
The beauty of it.

I'll stand for nothing less.
I won't suppress my mind,
It's flexing,
It's beating,
For rules
Created by someone else's
Flexing mind.
I'll surrender my body
To your rules,
But not my soul,
Contained in my mind.

Saturate yourself
With this thought.
Understand
This thought.
Accept this thought,
For it will never change.
Lay down your arms.
It can never threaten
My mind,
Another's mind,
Or their soul,
Or their state of being.

34 ("To Raneri, From Raneri")
I connect with it—
One level,
Only.
Bayside—
Anthony Raneri—
"So let's close our eyes
And we'll talk in the morning
When we're able to feel
The true weight of our words
And why we're both here.
And we can say we tried,
And take comfort in knowing
That if we both die alone
Tomorrow
That's the way that the stars aligned…"

It speaks to me,
To everyone,
In any situation
With any other person.
A universal aspect,
Yet personal—
To Raneri,
To me,
To you.

When he sings
I can see
The feeling in his eyes,
His brows.
I can feel
The feeling in his voice.

The words—
Basic,
But profound—

Understanding your words
So important.
Fate
And creating relationships,
Not understanding this
But just going with it.
Understanding—
Some don't work out,
But that everything works out for a reason—
The key to everything.

These words
Speak
To me,
To you,
To Raneri,
From Raneri.

35 ("Life and Loss")
I am the night runner.
Swift,
Inconspicuous,
Dodging all arms,
I reached immunity.
I REACHED IMMUNITY,
Then made it back to base camp
With *your* flag.
You couldn't stop me
Twice,
TWICE.
Think about that.
Our strategy—
Better,
At first.
But a draw—
That's how it ended.
Loss was never an option
For me.
A draw—
Loss.
But then—
A realization—
We suffer losses
To grow.
It's the only way
To grow.
Loss supports life.
Life supports loss—
An inseparable relationship—
From the beginning
To the end.

36 ("My Imitators")
Being a rebel—
Everyone wants to do it.
Why?
Being a rebel—
Trendy—
Which makes it
NOT rebellious,
NOT trendy.
Don't do it—
Just to be
"Cool,"
Just to
"Make a statement,"
Just to
"Piss someone off."
It's not worth it.
How do I know?
I've done it before,
Not once,
But twice—
Twice the time to learn the lesson—
It's just not worth it.
It...
Whatever that may be to you.

37 ("Competition Spirit")
Competitiveness—
Part of our human nature.
Why?
Why does one try to be better
Than another?
Cutting,
Pouring salt in the wound,
Never looking behind,
Just to be better
Than another.
For what?—
Glory?
That fades away
Over time.
I like to think—
Or cope
With competitiveness—
That we need it
To induce change,
And development,
To grow individually,
And together.
I want this to be true.
Convincing myself—
It's hard.
The pain caused to others in the process—
That's what is hard.
We need pain to grow.
But suffering—
No one wants that.
And loss of individuality—
No one wants that either.
Suffering,
Pain,
Competition,
Or

Sameness —
Your choice.

38 ("Independent Thinking")
People need to understand
THIS—
Thinking—
The greatest power of all.
Thinking for yourself,
Even better.
I can't think for you.
Stop asking me to.
Only you can do that.
I am human.
HUMAN—
Did you hear me?
I'm not
A hard drive.
I'm not
A flash drive.
I'm not
A memory card.
I am human,
Feelings and all,
Believe me.
So don't use me
For my mind
For your lack of effort,
And then discard me
When it's all over.
It just
Pierces me even more—
All the way to the core.

39 ("Fate")
I wonder—
Would I still be spending
Hours
With you,
Had fate
Not intervened?
I wonder—
Would I still be telling
Secrets
To you
That no one else knew,
Had fate
Not intervened?
I wonder—
Would I still be buying
Gifts
For you
That I never did
For anyone else,
Had fate
Not intervened?
I wonder—
Would I still be trying
To create
Something
That's not there,
Had fate
Not intervened?
I wonder
I wonder—
But wondering's over,
Thank God,
Because fate intervened.

40 ("Voids")
I do not want
Your _____.
Blank—
Unimportant.

I do not want
Your _____.
Blank—
Unimportant.

I do not want
Your _____.
Blank—
Important.
Bribes.
It said bribes.
Relationship.
It said relationship.

All I saw were _____ that day.
_____,
Running through my mind.
_____,
Still running through my mind.

I just want to _____ out.

41 ("Memory Reels")
Don't give me a camera.
Don't give me a journal.
Just give me music.
Let me walk silently
Observing,
And listening,
Capturing memories,
Recording them—
In the lyrics,
In the beats,
In the voice,
Of the artist.

Playback—
Special.
A moving picture
In my head,
Not just a stationary
Image.
The reel—
The music.
A living memory
With every play
Of the song.

It's something more special—
No one else can
See,
Or sense.
A personal possession.
The best possession
I could have.

42 ("Frustration")
Confused—
I am.
Frustrated—
I am.
Orphans—
I met.
Compassion—
I have
For everyone,
For orphans.
Compassion—
I don't have
For anyone,
Including orphans.

In context:
Circumstance—
Not *trying* to better yourself.
Not *caring* to try.
Living dependently,
Without a second thought.
Using me,
Manipulating me,
As if I was ignorant,
When I try to help.

Frustrated—
I am,
For *your* cause.

43 ("Revenge Not to Par")
No matter what I do,
It will never be up to par
With what you did.

I can try my hardest,
But I will never reach the state
That you reached—
It's not possible for me.

I am content in the phase
I am in,
No matter what.

I don't want to be you,
Reach your state ever—
That's the real lesson I learned
From your acquaintance.

44 ("Letter")
A lost letter
Never arrived,
Yet changed my life.
A phone call —
Result of
THE
Lost letter —
Placed me
Here,
In *THIS*
Time,
With you,
And others.

I said —
I wish
THE
Letter remained unknown.

I say —
I'm thankful
THE
Letter never arrived,
But made itself known.

45 ("Questions")
My foremost fear—
Death.
I wish I was prepared,
But I don't know
If anyone really is.
Rather—
People are ready
For the *anticipation*
Of death.

What scares me the most—
Not knowing
Where I'll go,
Whether I've been good,
Or bad,
How I'll pass,
Or when.

Me—
Not sure how
To prepare
For the anticipation
Of death.
Will I know I'm over
When it's over?

A girl died.
No one I knew.
But I ponder—
Does she know that she has died?
Did she know that she died?

But more so,
I ponder—
Why do we die?
Why is the right time

To die
When we die?

The only sure thing—
One day, *One day,*
I'll know the answers
To these immediate,
Unanswerable questions.

46 ("3 Foot Ledge")
The ledge—
Three feet above the ground.
I'm on the ledge.

I am scared of falling.
My balance—
Not good.
Even worse,
Now.

Hurricane winds—
Blowing every which way.
Pant legs like flags in the wind.
Hair like an untamed bush.
Arms outstretched like an eagle's wings.

Everything has stopped,
Except me,
In this moment,
Now.
I am scared of falling.
The wind—
Pushing me forward,
Arms floundering.

Falling forward—
The wind assisting,
Carrying me,
Continuing to push me
Even when I'm down.

Total loss of control.
Total chaos.
Can't get up,
But trying—
Adrenaline assisting me.

I love this.
I don't feel this often.
An unnerving situation,
But one I want to be in.

47 ("Emotional Drought")
I'm holding my conscious back
From thinking about
This emotional drought
I'm in.

It's better for me —
Being emotionless
Than
Emotional.
Stability occurs this way.

Memories blocked —
Specific feelings,
Specific times,
Specific people,
Obliterated.
My life —
Easier this way.
My life —
Less complicated this way.
My life —
Happier this way.

Happiness is —
Peace from
Emotion,
Memories.
Peace of
Mind,
Soul,
Body.
Peace for
Me.

48 ("Some")
Particle—
Enters nasal passage.
Receptors—
Bind particle.
Particle discharged,
Propelled back outwards,
But never forgotten.

I know—
If I never
Contact that particle again,
My nose will
ALWAYS
Remember it—
More so than any person.

That's good—
I'd rather remember
A smell,
Even bad,
Than some.

My nose—
Captures memories,
Carries memories.
Some—
Good.
Some—
Bad.
But all some—
Permanent.

49 ("Association")
Let's play a game.
I give words,
You associate:

Trust.
Sly.
Persistent.
Morals.
Compassion.
Pressure.
Priority.
Influence.
Authority.
Wrongdoing.
Power.

Many things come to mind—
Too overwhelming to handle.

Associate again,
Differently this time around.
That's what I am doing.

50 ("Finding Religion")
Everyone meets people.
I met a little girl,
Separated from me
By thousands of miles.
Of all people
She spoke to me the most—
She never did.
Most likely—
I'll never see her again
In my life.
But, I'll always remember her.
Language barrier—
Yes.
Underprivileged—
Yes.
But knowledgeable—
Yes.
She led
Me
To the House of the Gods.
I prayed my hardest there,
And received my prayers—
Especially,
Freedom from a guilty conscious.
She led me back.
I saw her one last time
Before I left,
But I never looked back—
I should have.

51 ("Departed")
You are leaving soon.
Will I ever see you again?
How much time will pass
Before I do?
Will things be
Different
Between us
This time around?
I hope so.
There's potential there.
You haven't completely given up.
I know.
I can see it in your eyes—
Reconciliatory.

You are leaving soon.
Will I ever see you again?
How much time will pass
Before I do?
Things will not be
Different
Between us
This time around.
I know so.
There's no potential there.
You have completely given up.
I know.
I can see it in your eyes—
Painfully glassy, cold.

52 ("Places I Want to Be")
My breath
Cutting air.
My feet
Stomping ground—
Crushing,
Breaking,
Fallen branches,
Roots.
Muscles flexing,
Pushing me forward.
Arms pumping,
Music in my ears.

Going uphill
Through hanging flowers
In trees,
Through sweetly smelling
Bushes,
Through patches of radiating
Sun,
Until reaching the top of a
Mountain
Overlooking a cliff—
Pure vegetation below.
Stopping,
Hands on knees,
Inhaling copious amounts of
Oxygen—
Flora all about me,
I look below me
At heavenly perfection.

I close my eyes,
Visualize it in my head.
I open my eyes—
Rise up,

Blinking,
Sweat dripping from my face.
People are passing me.
Shoes are squeaking on the courts.
Someone hits me to keep going.
It was never really there—
I must find this place.
It can't only exist in my mind—
Can it?

53 ("N. Face")
I admit—
My weakness—
Wanting material things.
Trendy,
The latest,
Material things.
Clarks,
North Face,
Nike,
Apple.
You name it,
I have it.
It's hard
For anyone
Not to *want* to be
Trendy.
But then I look,
And see
Those who want,
But can't have.
A feeling of
Depression,
Sadness,
Overcomes me.
Trendy
Goes out the window,
Becomes obsolete
In the face of more
Pressing issues.
My humanity
Arises,
Looms overhead,
Darkens the materialistic things
To a point
Where I no longer want them.
Maturity—

I've reached.
This realization—
Induced maturity.
There's no reverting now.

54 ("Remembrance")
Is anyone doing
What I am doing
Right now?
Who is thinking of me
Now?
Who is entering life,
Who is leaving life
In this moment?
We don't often
Take the time—
Think about minute things
Like this—
Think of others,
Their actions,
Unless…
It affects us.
A problem—
Yes.
Fixable—
I'm not sure.
Worried—
I am.
I must keep my focus—
Remember others—
Those
I know,
And don't.
Those
I forgot,
Who forgot me.
I must do it.
I don't know
For what reason,
But I must.

55 ("Internal Salad Bowl")
I am Hindu.
I am Indian.
I am American.
How much Hindu?
How much Indian?
How much American?
It's not important.
Parading it around —
A bad idea.
Let me be,
LET ME BE —
Just Indian,
Just Hindu,
Just American.

Should I feel bad
Expressing
My American ways?
I am equal —
Both American,
And Indian.
I don't speak
One of my native tongues.
But the other —
English —
Yes.
No scale of Indian-ness exists,
So let me be.
You can flaunt it,
Belittle your American-ness,
Yet live it too —
Hypocrisy.
But I refuse,
I refuse —
Not how I live.
I'll never live that way.

I am Indian.
I am Hindu.
I am American.
I am proud to be all.

56 ("Perceived Home")
It struck a note with me.
Why I hadn't noticed it earlier —
We don't see things that are
Good,
Right.

Stormy day —
Tornado hit later.
Hurricane winds,
Now.

Driving —
Dilapidated,
Standing,
White,
Pointed,
Fence —
Struck me.
I followed it.

At the center —
Rocks,
Moss growing between.
My eyes followed —
Cracked pathway,
Bushes outlining —
Perfectly cut,
Contrasting antique look.
Antique mansion —
Like out of *Forrest Gump*
Or Southern plantation setting.

Gone in a few seconds
But forever burned in my mind.
Who lives there?
I must possess that house when I'm older.

A treasure.
Someone's home.

Home is where the heart is.
I want my heart to be
THERE,
Someday.
My home,
One day.

57 ("Regeneration")
If organs could regenerate—
I would be growing a heart.
Previously—
Mine removed
In a sterile environment.
I was awake.
You were watching,
Heartless.
I saw everything—
A hole
Where my heart was.
You stole it,
Not out of love—
To be spiteful.
Never once thought of
Me,
My pain—
You caused.
I thought of yours—
I caused.
I trusted you.
You said
You loved me.
Then,
You hurt me.
You pretend like you
Did nothing wrong.
Give me my heart back!
I want my soul.
Soul and Heart,
Intertwined,
Can't live without each other.
I'm living without both,
Slowly growing them back.
You could
Show some heart—

You have two.
Release mine.

58 ("Caves")
The cave—
Dark,
Winding,
Twisting.
I'm running
Forward,
Looking back.
You—
Catching up,
Always been
The better runner.
My hands bound.
Very faint light—
Holes in rocks miniscule,
Teasing me
With little light.
I have no choice—
I must outrun you,
Not outwit you.

Your face haunts me—
Always has,
Always will.
I have to get away.
My fear—
You will never stop
Chasing me,
Haunting me.

59 ("Blue Sky")
Children ask—
Why is the sky blue?
Adults mislead
With their answers.
Just say—
Air molecules
Scatter sunlight,
Making it polarized.
Shorter wavelengths
At the blue end
Scatter most effectively—
Why the sky is blue,
In conjunction with
God's work.
It's not hard.
Children aren't ignorant.
Adults are
Ridiculous, sometimes.
Untruthful answers,
For what?
Children—
Smarter than adults, sometimes.
Let's not undermine them.
The truth should prevail—
Even why the sky is blue.

60 ("Screaming Capillaries")
My capillaries—
Connect my body,
Head to toe.
Blood rushing,
Furiously pumping.
I can't feel.
I can't see.
I only know—
So microscopic,
Yet supporting,
Sustaining,
My body,
My life.

When I scream
My capillaries scream.
When I breathe
My capillaries breathe
We are in sync,
Complete symbiosis.
I would never take away
One—
Ruining symbiosis.

My capillaries beat
Together
Now.
Throbbing,
Pulsing,
Together
Now.
Cohesiveness—
Essential
Between capillaries,
Between capillaries and me,
Between microscopic and macroscopic,

Between everything—
The key to success,
The key to progression,
The key to life,
It must be.

61 ("Morgues")
Something gruesome—
Wanting
To go to the morgue,
Wanting to see dead bodies.
I'm mesmerized—
Seeing death
In the physical form.
Unknown people—
Wondering
How they died,
When they died,
Their names,
Their history,
If they are connected to
Someone I know.
Wondering,
Never asking,
Keeping some mystery.
Are normal people
Like me?—
Wanting to go to the morgue?
Fascinated by the morgue?
Or
Am I just abnormal?—
The future doctor in me kicking in?

62 ("Water")
Water—
Sustains life—
Some more
Than others.
It was *my* water.
A girl stole it
From me.
She didn't run,
She didn't walk,
Away.
She stood there,
Just stood
Looking at me,
Speaking.
I couldn't understand.
I saw—
Poverty,
Sadness,
Sickness.
What did she want
From me?
Help—
No.
Water—
No.
I couldn't give her anything.
I wanted to.
What she wanted the most—
Some attention,
From someone who cared.
I cared then,
I still care now—
Eight years later.

63 ("Connectionless")
I've made the connection.
No.
I've realized the connection—
Things don't have to connect
To be beautiful.
Marcel Duchamp—
No connection,
No interpretation,
Just simple,
Just beautiful.
The Shins,
Phantom Limb—
Singing lyrics—
Not comprehensible,
No connection to the
Music, which is
Complex.
Music video—
A blur,
Confusing.
All three
Fuse together
To connect,
To be beautiful.
Separate them—
No link.
It's the most subtle connection,
Yet the most challenging,
Engaging.
I've made the connection
With this connection.
It's beautiful.

64 ("I.D.")
Rustling sounds.
Desks moving.
People coughing,
Breathing heavily.
I stare at the lecturer.
But like sound waves
Needing a medium
To move through,
Not functional without,
I see his mouth moving,
But no medium
Carries his sound to me.
I should care—
Body defense mechanisms,
Drug interactions,
Infectious diseases—
It directly
Affects me.
Yet,
I am distracted.
Distracted by—
Making an organization,
Thinking of my grades,
Will I be invited to a gathering—
All futile things,
All things that depend
On my health.

My health—
I take for granted.
Don't notice,
Until I am sick.
Opposite of futile—
Important.
I need to find
That medium,

Listen to his
Sounds,
Understand the risks
To my health.
If I don't—
I should forget
All futile things,
Things I want
To do,
Want to have.

Health—
Number one importance.
Everything else—
Futile.
A point easily missed...
By me,
By everyone.

65 ("Zoning Out")
Tiredness
Sweeps over me.
Peeling my eyes open—
A challenge.
Love Song—
311—
Playing.
Its reggae vibe,
His mellow voice,
The lyrics—
I'm in a trance.
He's reconfirming
My morals
With every word
He sings—
Piercing my heart.

I'm running
Through a
Golden field,
Sundress on,
Wheat blanketing me,
Hands brushing through
Stalks as I run.
He's singing
"However far away
I will always love you....
Whatever words I say,
I will always love you,
I will always love you."
I'm sitting at a
Willow tree,
Hearing
"Whenever I'm alone with you,
You make me feel like I'm home again."
I'm mellow,

Absorbing everything.
Sun setting,
Giving a rustic look to all in its path.
My eyes close
To the riffs
Of the guitar.

I awake—
Sitting in front of
My computer.
Papers surround me.
I'm enclosed in a tiny room.
This is reality.
That was peace.

66 ("D4")
I live
In a soundless place.
I'm walking.
All I hear—
Trees swaying,
Grass shifting,
Birds chirping.
I think—
Is it this quiet
Anywhere else
Right now?
Can it ever be
This quiet
In such places—
New York,
Philadelphia,
Boston?

Fate—
Put me in this place.
Why?—
Am I destined to be
Stuck here forever?
For how long?
I need more—
More sounds,
More interaction,
Just more—
From the environment,
From others,
From everything,
Satisfaction hasn't been reached…
Yet.

67 ("Revel")
I'm beat down,
Almost to the point
Of breaking,
To the point
Of quitting completely.

I'm beat down
By others,
By letting myself
Be this way.
You like to revel
In my grief,
My loss,
My failures,
As if
You were
Superhuman,
Supernatural.
Let's turn the table—
Your loss,
Your grief,
Your failures—
I would never revel in.
Think about that
Before you belittle me,
My soul.

We learned—
Treat others
Like you want to be treated—
Hypocrisy—
We don't follow.
Stop teaching this,
Making things worse.

People

Like me
Get hurt the most—
I can't seem to catch
A break.
Throw me a bone,
Throw me anything
God.
Help me out.
I need you,
Your help the most
Now—
A time of sadness—
Feelings of
Not
Being good enough,
Never will be—
The worst.
Help me overcome,
Be strong,
Combat others,
Harsh words,
Actions,
Please.
Please.
I need *You*
To help *me*
Now.

68 ("Connections")
Sitting here—
Making connections
Between words
And images,
I lose my
Competitive nature.
Don't care,
Except to better
My nature
For my sake,
Not for anyone else's.
Exploring my mind,
How I think,
How others
Perceive things
In a different light.

Human nature
At its best—
Conflicting minds,
Breeding argumentation,
Helping our minds grow,
Develop into
Something else.
I know
I'll be different
When I leave this room,
This atmosphere,
At least
Until
I return to reality.

69 ("Holding Time")
Time—
Slowing down.
I can feel it.
Like trudging through mud.
Should it speed up?—
It won't.
I don't know if I want it to.
But not slow either—
Just be normal.

Life without time—
Impossible.
It exists
Without numerical values,
By rotation of the planets—
Can't be stopped.

A concept—
Time—
So widely accepted,
Yet not explored,
Just taken for granted.
I'm only thinking
Of it now
For lack of occupation
With other things.
Time dominates
Everything.
Nothing will change that
Ever.
It's the one linking force
Between everything
Past—
Time—and
Present—
Time— and

Future—
Time.

70 ("Liberate Me")
My downfall—
I should have seen
It coming.
Good things
Always end
Badly,
For me—
Of my own fault.
Seen from another perspective—
What if
Things
Went correctly?
I wouldn't
Be happy,
Still—
It will never
Work out.
It took me
A while
To realize this,
But finally I did—
Shedding my selfish nature
To liberate myself—
Not a good feeling,
But one I had
To do,
To live life—
Myself.
Freely.

71 ("Burning Hope")
Hope
Burns in me—
Mysterious,
Ever pervading
My being.
It can't be rid of—
Not in me.
I've been defeated
Too many times,
Wanting to shed *all* Hope,
But can't.
Frustrating—
Hope keeps
Me trying
When I don't want to
Try.
I'd rather it burden me
Than be gone forever
Though.
Life without Hope—
No life at all.
Hope teases,
Hope deceives,
Hope keeps us going,
Moving forward,
Moving eternally.

72 ("Motion City")
I think—
I am writing—
Why?
For what reason?
Just to write—
No.
That's never the reason.
To make a statement—
No.
My life—
Changed drastically
In such a short time,
Hitting me
Like a semi
Blowing dust up from the road.
I'm on the side—
Dust in my eyes.
I'll always remember—
Never stand to close
From this experience.
I must document
All,
Vaguely,
Leave room for interpretation—
Just as time embellishes.
Memories
I can't forget,
I won't forget,
I don't want to forget—
An essential phase
In my life.
Writing—
Is forever.

73 ("Anchors Afloat")
Rise above—
What I want
To do.
Persevere—
What I want
To do,
Amidst obstacles
Carried on
My shoulders,
Weighing me down,
Weighing my soul down.
Time—
That's what it will take.
Time heals all wounds...
Right?
I believe—
I have to—
To keep going.
If I stop—
Time stops—
I can't let that happen.
Never.

74 ("Wars")
A war exists
Between opinions—
Who will dominate?
Moral disease—
Who will fix it?
We need—
Cleansing of the heart,
Cleansing of the mind,
Repentance
For evil thoughts,
Freedom
From a guilty conscious,
Repentance
From everyone,
Freedom
For everyone
To live a healthy life,
To rebel
Against shackles
Binding out spirits,
To choose well
Individually,
Not corporately,
To fill empty holes
In our lives,
To exhale freely,
And
Breathe clean air
For our bodies,
For our minds,
For our souls,
For our spirits.

75 ("Run to You")
So terribly
Ironic—
Me listening to a speaker—
Cardiologist—
Hours later—
I hear—
A loved one
Of someone I know
Passed away—
Cardiac related.

I'm shocked—
I didn't know him.
I still care.
Death—
A caring matter,
No matter who.
Death—
So cruel,
Cruel in its unexpectedness.

I was brought
Back to reality,
Put in my place,
Saddened.
My heart goes out to you—
Friend.

I want to run,
Run to you,
You who betrayed me.
I'm not sure why.
Memories—
Me telling you
The most important,
Pressing

Issue.
You not caring.
You won't remember.
I always will—
You said to the effect—
It's not that important.
You hurt me the most.

I want
To run
To you
Now,
In hopes
You will care
This time.
But I can't.
Facts exist—
The fact—
You won't care.
You never will.
It pains me
To realize this.
But,
Just as death is a fact,
So is your lack of care.
I will never come to
You
Ever again—
A fact.

76 ("Completion")
I was talking today
To a friend.
I said
Shockingly,
"Completion—
Lacking in my life."

Like the last piece to a puzzle,
Finding the needle in the haystack,
Opening the lock with the key,
I had a realization.
A realization—
Doesn't occur often—
I need
I must
Begin to complete things.

Beginning—
Priority for ending.
Beginning—
A physical task,
Not mental.
Ending = completion,
Also a physical task.

I—
Mental.
I—
Physical?
A change must be induced,
Turn mental to physical,
Turn thinking into doing.

77 ("Southern Girl")
Driving today—
Equivalent to freedom.
Sun beating down,
Incubating my long, black hair,
My wheat brown skin.
Breeze permeating
My eyes,
My face,
My neck,
The space between my fingers.

Endless stretches of
Open highway.
One side—
Grassy fields,
Creeks,
Swamps.
The other side—
Alabama farm lands,
Horses,
Water wheels,
And one billboard—
"Go to church or…"
The rest—
Self-explanatory.

Peaceful,
Simple,
Beautiful.
The highway—
Sign of
Progression,
And character.

Yet…

Every time—
Catches me
In a trance,
In a surprise—
The confederate flag.
Huge—
Its size,
Its flowing movements,
Its presence,
And,
What it stands for—
A sign of regression
Amidst progression,
A sign of turmoil
Amidst peace—
But only for some.
For others—
A sign of progression
Amidst regression,
A sign of peace
Amidst turmoil.

I remain neutral,
My heritage uninvolved—
At least,
What I tell myself.
No thoughts
On this statement,
Except—
It's best not to think about
Symbols,
Cloth flags.
Just drive
I think—
To it,
Past it,
Two seconds,

And then
Return to normality—
Farms,
Sunny days,
Music,
Dreams,
Southern history.

78 ("Burdened Mind")
I think—
Every moment
Of every day—
Like everyone else.

I feel,
I know,
I think
On a heightened level—
No arrogance involved,
No boon—
Dwelling on words—
A punishment.

Words—
Receiving,
Processing,
Analyzing,
Analyzing...
Nonstop—
Racking my mind,
Distracting me from
The complete picture,
The complete idea.
I'm missing,
Missing the point,
Missing the point—
Missing life,
Word by word.

How to make it stop—
An enigma
To myself.
Others—
Oblivious to *my* plight.

Stop thinking—
Like burning bridges—
Not an option.
Think less—
My conscious
Controls itself.
Losing control—
Yes.
I can't keep up—
My life—
Consumed
By words.

Writing—
Controlling words—
Choosing,
Rearranging,
Laying them out.
I'm in control
For once,
Over my conscious—
The only time.

I must—
Always—
Keep writing.

79 ("Sink")
I stood
Posed
In front of the mirror.
I stood
Staring
At the sink below.

Is it true—
Hot,
Steaming
Water
Washes away
Dirt,
Germs,
Guilt?

My hands—
Nerves past pain threshold,
Feeling nothing,
Under gushing,
Hot
Water.
Heat meter broken.
I stare—
Reddening hands,
Prune withered.
Ridges in my hands—
A glimpse of old age.
Has guilt been sucked out
Of my skin,
My being—
Evidence provided by withered skin?

I stare—
The mirror,
My face—

Deceiving my hands.
My face—
Shows no guilt,
Not even the eyes.
My hands—
Show all guilt.

I've washed it away
For now.
Guilt—
Like a chronic disease,
Returning when
My hands heal,
Until they face the
Wrath of cleansing
Again.

You'll see me—
Washing my hands
Nonstop—
Temporary freedom,
But a slave to the sink,
Washing away
Fifteen minutes of infamy
In a lifetime of
Boiling water.

80 ("Assembly Line Produced")
Untie me
Completely.
Release me
From all obligations—
To be me.

I am the same
As you,
As the next,
As the future—
All assembly line productions.

Don't you see?—
All doing the same,
Every moment,
Every second,
Thinking the same—
An unhealthy gesture,
For us,
For others.

I'm jumping
Off the assembly line,
Sure to be stopped.
By others—
No.
By myself—
Yes.
Why?
My aspirations—
Generic,
Assembly line produced—
Inside the box.
Inside the circle.
Whatever,
Just not

Outside—
The most important.

I'm stuck,
Trapped
Inside the box
By my own
Generic
Aspirations—
Only achieved through
Conformity.
I don't want conformity,
Average-ness.

I want me!
I want me!
For me,
For others.

81 ("Living")
Someone once said—
"The moment we are born,
We are dying."
I agreed...
For a moment.
Why so negative?
Why not
"The moment we are born,
We are living." –
Living.

It's true—
The first thing
Contacted in life—
Bacteria.
We don't think of this.
We shouldn't.
We think—
We should think—
Life is born.
Glory,
Success—
All to come in the future.

Aging—
No indication of death,
But a sign of experience—
Experience a sign of living.

Let life take its course.
Next time
I'll say
"The moment we are born,
We are living."

82 ("Recoil for You")
Physics—
Taught me about
Recoil—
The principles of recoil.

My heart—
Recoils—
Pulsating against
My ribs,
My skin.
When still—
Completely—
It's unnerving—
Feeling,
Seeing
This recoil.

My heart—
Wants to burst through,
Free itself—
I think sometimes.
Other times—
My heart,
Complacent where it is.

Recoil increases
When I see
You.
Anxiety sweeps over me,
Drowning me—
I hide.
Recoil decreases
When you disappear.

I hate recoil
Then.

I love recoil
Now.

83 ("Blank Space")
I sit
Here
Now.

The only things moving—
My hair,
My heart,
And
My mind.

I want
To think
Here,
Now.
It's hard,
I'm forcing myself—
Not something I want to do.
I just want
Natural,
Free-flowing thought,
Like all other moments in my life
Except
Here,
Now.

84 ("Stranger")
The girl across from me—
No one I know—
Brown hair,
Almost black,
Like my own.
Sunglasses on,
Shielding her eyes
From me,
From the world,
Like I want to do
Sometimes.
Smiling.
Why the smile?—
Not one of
Arrogance or
Mischievousness,
But one of
Complacency.
What is she thinking?
I will never know.
I believe
Or
I want to think
The book she's reading—
Purple,
Orange,
Black,
Brown,
Title unknown,
Too far for my eyes to know—
Is causing the smile.

I hope on day
She reads
Paper Words and Paper Hearts—
My own,

Smiling,
Understanding myself,
Even if I never
Understand her
Or
Know her.

85 ("Black Balloon")
A child holds
A Black Balloon,
Holding another child's hand.
Both smiling.
What is the fascination with
The Black Balloon?
Is it because it
Defies gravity,
So dark it's almost colorless?
I walk by,
Stare at them,
The Black Balloon.

I realize—
I am thinking about
The Black Balloon,
They are not.
My fascination—
From experience.
Theirs—
Pure feeling,
Naiveté.

I think of
Helium,
Composition of atoms,
Rubber,
Dyes—
Over thinking.

They think—
It's a Black Balloon.
Simply—
A transient object,
To be enjoyed now
Because when it's gone

There will be no
Second thought of
Its existence.

86 ("Evaluation Form")
I need to
Revaluate—
My life.
Mostly—
My conscious.

Unproductive thoughts—
Festering in
My head,
Killing my
Brain
Slowly,
Like a chronic infection.

A cure—
What I need.
It must be out there—
Not elusive,
Like the cure for cancer.

The worst part—
They go away,
Teasing me,
Until their return.
A nonstop process.

I wonder—
Does anyone else
Have a conscious
Like mine?

87 ("Futures")
I believe in Futures.
I don't believe in Pasts
Or Presents—
A warped form of Pasts.

I don't live in the past.
I don't live in the present.

I live in the Future.
My future exists
Now,
Not in the present—
Through my
Closed eyes,
Dreams,
Thoughts.

I imagine
What I want,
On any level,
In any place,
At any time.

A lonely place.
Yet,
The only place
I want to be
Now,
Not in the present.
Now,
In the future.

88 ("Photographer")
I am not a photographer.
Yet, tonight—
I was a *professional* photographer—
Not because I wanted to be,
But because I was forced to be.

I was hidden
Behind the camera,
The camera more important than
Me,
My feelings.

You all know this.
Yet, you continue
To place me behind,
Not in front.

I'd rather be blinded by—
Flashes
Than—
Your vindictiveness.

Don't play with my mind.
Don't play with anyone's—
An unwanted,
Undeserved
Responsibility.

89 ("Paper Words and Paper Hearts")
Paper words
And
Paper hearts—
My surroundings
Right now.

I *want* substance.
I *need* substance—
To life,
To words,
And,
To hearts.

Are *my* words
Paper?
Is *my* heart
Paper?
I'd like to think not,
That for certain others—
Yes.
But,
I really don't know.

I *feel* a lot now—
More so than ever in my life—
I now know I *don't* have a paper heart.
I can't express the feelings,
Setting a standard,
A threshold.
If surpassed,
A subsisting heart,
Subsisting words.
If not,
A paper heart
And
Paper words.

I can't live with
Paper hearts
And
Paper words—
Simply,
It's not living.
Simply,
I want to live.

Give me more than that—
More than paper.
Give me being.
Give me subsistence.
Give me sustenance.
Just give me life
By denying

Paper words
And
Paper hearts.

90 ("Beginnings")
New beginnings,
Something I look forward to,
Anticipating the time
They will come.

Sometimes I think they will come.
Then an overwhelming sense
Tackles my spirit—
There are no new beginnings,
Just continuations of beginnings.

"It can't be,"
I tell myself.—
Time being tedious,
But it is so.

Tedious time leads to
Interconnected People,
Interconnected Places,
Interconnected Everything.

Severance is what I need
From connections.
Connections make continuations,
Severance makes beginnings.

Imagine beginnings,
How cleansing—
To the spirit,
To everything.

If beginnings are only imaginable,
Wake me when they become reality.

91 ("Battle with Myself")
Something is calling me,
Calling me back,
Tying me down.

It's my internal self—
My second being.

I want to run from it,
But I'm running towards it,
Assisted by a rope.

It's ironic—
I'm wanting to run from the same me
That's writing these words.

So I want to run from these words—
These words that I'm defining,
These words making these situations—
No.

See,
These words,
These situations,
Don't define me.
I define myself.

I will always be tied to my internal self,
Its words.
But only I can make me,
Only I can define myself—
Not by words,
Or situations,
But what I make of these same words
And situations—
By and *only* by who I basically am.

92 ("Break, Not Bend")
My mind is breaking,
Not bending.
My mind is super-saturated,
Not saturated.

I see my brain
Oozing from
My eyes,
My nose,
My ears,
But not my mouth,
As I am screaming.

Equilibrium is acting,
Doing a service to me—
Shifting from products to reactants,
From too much to too little,
From overworked to simply worked.

I just sit
And stare
Now.
No action,
No movements,
No thoughts.
I don't want to be like this,
But I can't change.
Change is not inevitable—
Not in this case.

93 ("Twice Strong Bond")
Today—
A life lesson learned,
In the span of less than
One minute.

It struck me,
Like some futile things.

Important things—
Don't impact me,
Until times later,
Usually.

Times later—
One hour,
One day,
One year,
At least.

The life lesson—
Friendship,
Based on trust,
Nothing else,
Struck me in the
Less than one minute span.

I was trusted today.
When I realized this,
I realized I had a friendship,
An important one,
One that I won't let go,
Like others I did.

Someone once told me,
It's ok to make a mistake once,
But not twice.

I've mistaken twice,
And now,
NO MORE.
I refuse.
I refuse.

I just wish people would believe me.
I believe myself.

94 ("Saved")
I'll never understand—
How one can take another's life.

A fundamental concept—
Learned from the youngest of years—
Treat one as you want to be treated.

This fundamental was lost,
Until this week.
How many lives must be taken to make us
Re-realize this fundamental?—
Double digits,
Digits too many.

Tears to my eyes,
To realize this,
The whole situation,
The isolation of it,
The universality of it.

I wish everyone
Would listen to my words,
Understand that senselessness is
Futileness,
That we can't be like this—
We must respect everyone,
No matter what the conditions
Of our lives—
We must treat others
As we want to be treated—
A simple concept—
Simple to grasp,
Only if we let ourselves.

95 ("Tell Me So")
I can see better days coming.
The smiles on the faces
Of those we love
Tell me so.
That's all I care about,
That's all I need to care about.

96 ("Two Feet")
I am tired of feeling bad—
I realized
I don't have to,
Not anymore.

I don't have to feel anything
Anymore—
That's how it goes
Now.
That's how it will be
From now on.

Even with less than two feet between,
I felt nothing—
I was liberated from that moment.

A year—
For me to be liberated.
A year—
Of feeling everything
When I didn't want to,
But forced to.
One—
Liberated from the beginning of the year,
Felt nothing...
Representative of the
Once false friendship—
Me feeling everything,
One—
Nothing.

I joined other ranks now—
I feel nothing,
At least not now.

97 ("Integrity Maintained")
I have come full circle—
I am seeing 20/20—
From the depths of darkness—
Coping with the cancer of my mother,
To dealing with two lost ones.

All have made me stronger,
Made me realize what I have,
That that's all I need,
And nothing more.

All have made me realize my mistakes,
Who I am,
Who I need to be,
And where I need to be.

I now ask myself—
"How can I maintain my integrity
On a daily basis,
To keep my integrity for life?"

I am still reeling from past mistakes
Like everyone else,
But I am turning them to corrections
And not faults—
That's all I can do,
That's all I'll ever be able to do,
That's all I want to do.

98 ("Bleeding Heart")
I don't have a paper heart—
My year of feelings has told me so.

I worried for a year—
That my heart was paper
And nothing else,
That I was leading an unresponsive life.

But today,
I can stand
And say
"My heart is
Not paper."

Today,
My heart
Is strength,
Is compassion,
Is resilience,
Is—
A heart,
A real heart,
Not a paper heart.

99 ("Weighted Words")
I don't use paper words—
My year of feelings has told me so.

I worried for a year—
That my words were paper
And nothing else,
That I was saying futile things,
Things I didn't mean.

But today,
I can stand
And say
"My words are
Not paper."

Today,
My words
Are real,
Are provoking,
Are me,
Are words,
Real words,
Not paper words.

100 ("Closure")
Closing something—
Always the hardest thing to do—
In relationships,
In words,
In minds,
In anything.
Closure doesn't come easy—
It takes work.

For me—
Six months of work—
Now closing in 100—
No words
Or feelings
Come to mind,
Or heart.

I thought I would be drowned
In emotion.
But, I am
Emotionless—
Floating.

I don't feel good,
I don't feel bad,
I don't feel anything.

So with these words,
And no thoughts,
No feelings,
I close a year of my life
In words
Written in six months.

That's all I have left to say.
Nothing more.

Additional Poems

101 ("Colorful")
We laugh because
We are colorful.

We laugh together—
Requiring at least two,
Physically,
Or in mind.

So don't feel alone—
Isolation is a state of mind,
A concept,
Nothing real.

The conscious
Of the mind
Makes separation
Impossible—
Separation of the soul
And body
Non-existent.

The clincher:
All minds intertwined,
A never changing concept,
Saturating our daily lives
With dependency,
And irreversibility.

It's making us—
Making us laugh
Because we are colorful.

102 ("Pushed Together")
We have become
One.
God is pushing us together—
At least I believe.

I'm caving in
Because I don't want to be
Forced into closter phobia—
Not with this many others.
I'm caving in
Because I want to,
Because I see resolution.

May resolution occur—
Like for so many others.

Becoming one cell—
Not many.
One cell—
Resistant,
Unwilling to give in,
Constantly changing
Together,
Changing in harmony.

103 ("Wraps")
There are nights where I dream.
There are nights where dreams are absent.
There are nights where dreams exist
But don't meet permanence.

I don't know which I prefer.
It's a saving grace to dream and see things,
Things I know I won't see in this lifetime.

Like wishes
Never shared with anyone
Or secrets
Too damning to tell,
But surviving,
I dream under wraps until
I wake in a crisis.

The crisis—
To make something happen,
To change things,
Things that are resistant to change
But not of their own will,
But because of mine—
My fear,
My reluctance,
My anger,
My frustration.

When this situation gets spread so thin,
So overrated,
I'll call forth dreams
To induce change.
But not now,
No matter how much
I desire it.

104 ("ER")
My soul cries out to you,
Even though vocally I want to resist,
Even though mentally I am not prepared.

My mind still trusts in private,
Not publicly.
It's hard for me—
Everyday a challenge,
To accept this loss,
A sort symbolic death,
One more so than the other.

I want the revival to occur,
Hope burning in my mind,
But decaying in my heart
With each block of time that goes by.

I sit in silence.
I want to prove my heart wrong,
But my mind is forfeiting
To its burning will.

Loss is learning—
I need this loss
To induce realization.
But I can't stop fighting—
It's not me,
Although I want it to be.

105 ("Green X")
Say something!
Say anything!
I don't care—
I just want some reversal of time,
Any second I can get.

The ink of the hand,
Too much for me
To deal with it.
I ran to the sink
Just to wash it off.
It wouldn't wash away.

For one day—
I stared at the ink,
The ink of memories,
The ink of connections,
The ink of all I didn't want.

I wanted to erase the history of writing
In that moment,
But I couldn't.
All I could do was be strong
And bear the ink with frustration.

The ink is just another memory now—
A memory that phases me still,
A memory that crosses time's boundaries,
Unrelenting and
Willingly.

106 ("Confusion")
I have never been so mentally drained—
Thinking of people,
Memories,
Things to do.

I've always known where to start and how.
Now, I am lost—
Not knowing where to start,
What to start,
How to start.

When I am confused—
Mentally,
Soulfully,
My mind recollects thoughts
I pushed back into the depths of my brain,
Thoughts I'd like to avoid.

I'd like to think the brain
Reads only surface material.
I keep my surface area saturated
With futile information.

I am running out of futile information.
My mind is tired of saturating itself—
It's letting uninvited thoughts back
To the surface
From tiredness,
And lack of effort.
I'm not resisting anymore.

107 ("Borrowed, Not Returned Feelings")
This music has entered my soul.
When I hear singing,
I am singing—
Capturing the emotion
In my body,
Especially in my head.

Once the emotion has pervaded my being
It stays forever.
It can be recalled
Whenever I feel the necessity.
It can be stored away,
Obliterated temporarily,
Whenever I feel the necessity.

What I can't put into
Words,
Emotions,
Feeling,
This music does for me.

My only regret
Stems from the fact that I am borrowing
Words,
Emotions,
Feelings,
Things that aren't mine,
And making them mine.
But it's the only way
To make expressionless times
Expressional.

108 ("Thank You")
I want to thank *you*
For being a part of my life.
You made me realize
More than *you*'ll ever know,
More than *you*'ll ever realize.
Thank *you*.

109 ("Inside Explosion")
It's time to escape.
The feeling of being trapped
Overwhelms me.

I just want to scream,
Throw things,
Punch things,
My mind can't breathe!

I've reached the maximum point.
It's over.

At this moment,
The vessels in my brain are pulsing.
I feel like they want to explode.

All the adrenaline is rushing,
But I'm just sitting.
I don't know what to do,
But wait for the end to come.

It's so close,
Too close,
So that time slows down.
It can't—
Not when I need it this much.

110 ("Year Day Later")
April 29, 2006.
What were you doing?

I know what I was doing—
Being impulsive.

April 29, 2007
What will you be doing?

I know what I will be doing—
Being rational.

A year later—
Just one.
In just one short year,
I have come a long way,
Everyone has.

I can't relate to others,
Only myself.
I only know myself.
I know others in relation to myself.

I am trying to give you a glimpse
Of who I am,
My most internal self.
This is the closest I can get,
You can get,
Without being me.

That's all I can offer you.
Take it.
Don't leave it.

111 ("Judgment")
Certain words just pervade
All thoughts.

Someone said to me today
"It's not my place to pass judgment,
Only God's."
These words
Hit me so hard
In an indescribable way.

I stopped,
I analyzed,
Myself.

I thought:
How can I stop passing judgment?
Can it be stopped?
Is it a fatal human flaw?

Then I realized—
I should only pass judgment on myself,
Not others.
Do this and be constructive.

Everyone is judgmental,
Consciously or not.
But not everyone is constructive.

Judging can't be stopped.
It's in God's hands.
It's in our hearts to be responsible
By being consciously constructive.

Fin